PERSONAL GROWTH AFFIRMATIONS

PAMELA CUMMINS

Copyright © 2018 by Pamela Cummins

All rights reserved. No part of this publication may be reproduced, distributed, or transmitted in any form or by any means, including photocopying, recording, or other electronic or mechanical methods, without the prior written permission of the publisher, except in the case of brief quotations embodied in critical reviews and certain other noncommercial uses permitted by copyright law.

Cover Design by Brent Meske

ISBN-13: 978-0-9976703-2-5

*Dedicated to those courageous enough
to journey upon the personal
growth path…*

INTRODUCTION

When I began writing entries for this book, *Personal Growth Affirmations*, back in January 2017, my intentions were to create fifty-two weekly love affirmations. Each week I allowed my Angels and guides to dictate the topic for the week that I placed on my *love affirmation* website page. During the course of the year, it became apparent that the love affirmations were actually about personal growth. This makes sense, for the more you reach your highest potential, the easier it is to attract a high level partnership that continues to grow...

This book was originally written to read at the beginning of the year for a weekly affirmation; nonetheless, you can choose to use it differently. For instance, you could: begin the book at any time, read the book from the end to the beginning, close your eyes while you scroll to a page, or read an affirmation every day for fifty-two days. Please utilize this book in whatever manner feels right to you. For your information, week one, seven, and fifteen's affirmations were written especially for the New Year's, Valentine's Day, and spring cleaning. Yet, you can express love daily, and clean or start a new year at any time.

As you work toward reaching beyond your current limitations, your life will metamorphose in ways you can't fathom today. This has proven true for me as well. Since I have been consciously on the personal/spiritual growth journey since November of 1989, I've seen my life and relationships transformed into an awesome masterpiece. We humans have the ability to truly manifest Heaven on Earth if we chose to journey upon the personal growth path.

Are you ready to begin?

WEEK ONE

A NEW YEAR, A NEW YOU

We, as people, find happiness and fulfillment when we strive to reach our full potential during our lives on planet Earth. Think of human beings as beautiful diamonds that need to be polished every day. When we are born our diamond selves are crystal clear; it is society's fears, beliefs, and judgements that dull and block our clear essence from shining through. Which is why we must increase our self-love, work on our personal growth, expand our spirituality, and push on towards our life goals.

In this New Year, who do you want to become? What do you need to let go of that is no longer working in your life? How would you like your life to be next year?

Today is the day you can take the steps

to the life you always imagined! This is not an overnight process, there is no time limit; for we are always a work in progress. Baby steps are the way to go to achieve a new you. The first step is to write, type, sing, draw, paint, or create a vision board of big goals for the year. You may want to break down each goal into smaller doable steps. Each day you can do one or more undertakings toward your goals.

. . . .

I am allowing my diamond self to become clearer to expand into who I truly am and can become.

. . . .

WEEK TWO

I AM WHO I AM

Has anyone ever made fun of you for being who you are? Did they insult your appearance? Were you told that your dreams and goals are impossible and would never happen? Welcome to the human race. Everyone has experienced not being accepted for who they are. At times, you may be the one who is not accepting something about the person who is criticizing you or an aspect of another individual.

When someone does not embrace you for who you are, they are showing you who *they* actually are. The criticizer is looking at you, yet really seeing a reflection of themselves. You are reflecting how they don't know and like themselves. The person is not satisfied with their appearance, nor do they believe they'll ever achieve what is truly within their heart. You may have experienced being the victim of a criticizer, but you also may have insulted others.

The criticizer and victim are both roles we play to learn to accept who we truly are – beautiful beings of love and light working toward our higher potential. Today is the day to be who you are, despite the opinions of others. Now is the time to stop viewing others' fault, instead start to look within, and begin to accept who you are. Everyone is weird; therefore, let us allow our weirdness to shine!

．．．．．．．．．．．．．．．．．

I am who I am, others are who they are, and we are all on our path to blossoming into our highest divine selves.

．．．．．．．．．．．．．．．．．

WEEK THREE

BE NICE TO YOURSELF

Once upon a time, I was in a course where a woman said to our teacher, "I have no trouble doing nice things for other people, but I just can't seem to do that for myself." The teacher was pondering the answer, when I blurted out my two cents, "Pretend you are someone else." Our teacher smiled and agreed with my feedback. Are you like that woman in being nice and taking care of everyone else, yet not yourself? You deserve kindness just like everyone else.

You are as valuable as the people you take care of, whether it is your parents, children, love partner, boss, co-workers, employees, or customers. You matter! We are all children of God, Goddess, Universe, or whatever you choose to call it. In this higher power's eyes everyone is equally important and deserves love and kindness.

From now on, be as nice to yourself as

you are to others. Here are some ways you can be nice to yourself: think and talk kindly about yourself, take care of what you have to do *before* you take care of some else's needs, and say no to something you don't want to do. Do what you love and brings you joy, enjoy a hobby, listen to your favorite song, watch your favorite movie, or take a nap. Please continue to add what feeds your soul onto this list…

. . . .

I am nice to myself and every day I will take one or more kind action for myself.

. . . .

WEEK FOUR

YOU ARE AN IMPORTANT AND VALUABLE PERSON

Did a parent or authority figure tell you that you would never amount to anything or your goals were wrong? Their opinion has nothing to do with you and really is all about their doubts, fears, and insecurities. There is a reason you're on the Earth; thus you're NOT worthless.

Your role is to use your unique gift to help improve society. Whether you are a banker, teacher, artist, doctor, healer, author, psychic, musician, actor; or whatever that deep calling inside of you is. You may try to deny it by claiming you don't recognize what it is. Yet, you do know. What makes you happy, brings you peace, or you would do it for free? That is your vocation.

Learning to be nice to yourself is doing what makes your heart sing, despite other people's opinions. Start small and go big with your calling: enjoy it in your free time, engage in doing it part time, and advance to full time. Believe in yourself, walk through your doubts, and create your destiny!

••••••••••••••••••

I'm an important and valuable person that benefits the planet.

••••••••••••••••••

WEEK FIVE

YOUR BETTERMENT ENCOURAGES OTHERS

Your life will improve when you discover your goals, are kind to yourself, and do your important work on the planet. Because of this, your revelation will aid others in becoming who they are supposed to be. Wouldn't you like your life to keep improving and benefit other peoples' lives?

It doesn't matter what stage you are at in your life's journey; there will always be someone you admire who is ahead on a similar path. Just as there is someone behind you who admires your current position in life. Neither spot is better; instead what counts is perseverance on the adventure no matter what is thrown at you.

When you help and encourage others on their journey, it also propels you further on your own course. Treating others nicely and aiding them to know they are important and valuable reminds you to continue to do that for yourself. Your betterment assists *their* growth. Their growth increases *your* betterment.

· · · · · · · · · · · · · · · · ·

I am working on myself and goals, so it may ripple out to encourage others to do the same.

· · · · · · · · · · · · · · · · ·

WEEK SIX

INCREASE YOUR SELF-LOVE

Do you complain that you are all alone? Are you concerned regarding what your mate will do for you? Those are secondary problems. Rather than focusing on I'm all alone or what am I getting, focus on self-love.

Self-love attracts *higher love*! When you look outside to be loved, the energy you are sending out could be: neediness, anger, fear, jealousy, competition, frustration, sadness, moodiness, insecurity, impatience, greed, or dominance. You will receive weak love with that type of vibration.

Every morning ask yourself, "What can *I do* for myself that would increase my self-love?" Then do it, whether that's listening to your favorite song ten times in a row, wearing clothes that make you feel wonderful, or eating healthy food. Keep doing this, maintaining self-love, while observing how the world responds.

. . . .

I am increasing my self-love, which automatically attracts higher love from others.

. . . .

WEEK SEVEN

GIVE LOVE ON VALENTINE'S DAY

Many moons ago, I was alone on Valentine's Day. I felt heavy hearted and binged on mega amounts of chocolate and candy. That made matters worse. Boy, did my tummy ache! May you learn from my lesson not to stuff emotions through gluttonous eating.

If you're feeling disappointed in regards to Valentines' Day, know that you have the strength to turn discontentment into love. Allow yourself an hour of the blues by using a timer: cry, journal, pound a pillow, yell, or confide in someone safe. Once the timer rings, it's time to get off the pity pot.

Think of ways you can spread the love. You could buy candy and/or a box of Valentines' cards to give to people at work, family members, friends, or clients. Volunteer and give service to animals or people in need. Give yourself the gift of self-love by getting a massage or other form of pampering. Send out the love energy through intention and meditation.

· · · · · · · · · · · · · · · · ·

I am giving love on Valentine's Day and every day.

· · · · · · · · · · · · · · · · ·

WEEK EIGHT

RESENTMENTS BLOCK LOVE

Do you feel wronged by someone? Are you still blaming that person for ruining your life? Whoever you're resenting has moved on and might have forgotten about the incident that wounded you. Or perhaps, they are haunted by guilt.

You had no control over their past actions, nor how they feel about it. What you do have control over is how you choose to respond to it. One choice is to hold on to the resentment, although this will create barriers in your heart. The second choice is to find the lesson in the stunt they pulled and choose to grow from it.

Your resentment has only injured yourself by creating obstacles to love and joy. Wouldn't you like more happiness and loving relationships in your life? Take the baby steps to letting go of your grudge by getting into the *feeling* underneath – anger, disappointment, sadness, and deep hurt. Let go of why you think the person did you wrong. Instead, acknowledge that people who are hurting inside will turn around and hurt others to ease their pain. Do your best to see what this event has taught you and become willing to begin the process of forgiveness.

I am choosing to let go of resentments that are holding me back from love.

WEEK NINE

BEGIN THE FORGIVE-NESS PROCESS

Having a resentment against someone hurts *you*. Blaming a person for ruining your life wounds *you*. Feeling depressed over what happened harms *you*. The past is over, now is the time to begin anew. Forgiveness helps pave the way to a better future.

Some events in your life will be easier to forgive: a person steps on your toes, a co-worker makes you look inferior at a meeting, you catch a friend in a white lie, a cashier short changes you, your pet vomits on the carpet, and so forth. These occurrences happen every day, will not matter in a week, and are easy lessons in basic 101 forgiveness.

Other predicaments are more difficult to forgive: a co-worker steals your work and obtains a promotion, a drunk driver kills a loved one, you are a victim of crime, your spouse has an affair, you get raped, and anything else that can bring on post-traumatic stress disorder. These events are not something you just get over, for that would be denial. Instead, give yourself the gift of taking baby steps toward the goal of forgiveness.

· · · · · · · · · · · · · · · · ·

I am willing to begin the forgiveness process.

· · · · · · · · · · · · · · · · ·

WEEK TEN

THE FORGIVENESS JOURNEY

Congratulations on the courage to start the forgiveness path! The first step is to acknowledge your feelings and process them in a healthy manner. You can do this by writing in a journal, allowing the tears to fall, cursing like a sailor, punching a punching bag, or talking to a person who is safe. Dealing with your feelings, instead of stuffing them, prepares you toward the final result of forgiving.

Allow time – time. For forgiveness doesn't work on a schedule. Continue to allow whatever thoughts or feelings to come up. Do not make matters worse by taking vengeful actions, in the long run, these will boomerang to harm you. Instead, close your eyes to visualize telling off the person who harmed you or throwing balls of white light at them. You could even put yourself in their shoes going through a horrific time in their life to enable you to behold their humanness.

Pray and/or wish them well, even if you need to fake it. Look for the lesson of what this event is teaching you since everything does happen for a reason. You are learning to forgive them to release the past and create freedom toward a well-lived future life. You don't need to break bread with whoever harmed you, nor forget their actions. When you least expect it, you will be able to forgive fully.

. . . .

I am starting the forgiveness process to bring freedom and peace into my life!

. . . .

WEEK ELEVEN

START A JOURNAL

Journaling is always recommended in different therapies and self-help groups to assist an individual with their personal and spiritual growth. One of the most important purposes of a journal is that it aids taking whatever is on your mind out of your head and onto paper. This helps to relieve feelings, to stop obsessing over something, to prevent an outburst with another person, or to choose healthy actions.

Decades ago, I decided to try this journaling thing, bought a beautiful notebook, wrote a couple of a paragraphs, and noticed I misspelled a few words. My inner perfectionist jumped out of bed, grabbed the dictionary off my bookshelf, and began to thumb through it to find the word's correct spelling. Before I could even find the word, it occurred to me that this journal was for *me*. It didn't matter what or how I wrote it due to the fact that no one was ever going to read it. Why should I care if a word were misspelled? If anyone ever snooped in my journal, they wouldn't be able to understand my errors, which made my journal even more private.

Your journal is exactly that - your journal to do what feels right to you. Here are some suggestions: write a letter to God, the Angels, or to a deceased loved one. You could make turn it into a diary of your daily events. Use it to answer questions from a self-help book. Doodle, color, or compile sketches. Create a list of goals with the steps needed to achieve your heart's desire. Or allow your feelings to come up while journaling until they have dissipated.

• • • • • • • • • • • • • • • • •

I am keeping my journal as a secret and special place to do whatever I choose!

• • • • • • • • • • • • • • • • •

WEEK TWELVE

CONNECT WITH YOUR HIGHER SOURCE

Your higher source can be whatever you desire it to be or choose to name it, which could be: God, Goddess, Great Spirit, Buddha, Jesus, oneness, angels, the universe, nature, or love. Since this is your personal connection, other people's opinions, religions, or dogma are not included, nor allowed in this partnership.

Your special relationship with your higher source is the interaction that happens according to what feels right in the moment. You may pray, communicate quietly, laugh, tease, complain, holler, and allow the tears to flow. How you behave is your choice for the reason that this is your personal union.

How can that be? Your partnership with your higher source is a divine relationship where it is safe to be whom you truly are.

However, you may believe it doesn't know what you're thinking and whatever actions you took. It already knows; therefore, your sharing of yourself is a courtesy to a source who already loves you.

. . . .

I am connecting with my higher source who accepts me completely.

. . . .

WEEK THIRTEEN

TURN OVER YOUR PROBLEMS TO YOUR HIGHER SOURCE

Do you attempt to solve all your problems by yourself? Have you ever stayed up all night over analyzing an issue? Did you make yourself ill over this dilemma? Stop banging your head against the wall attempting to locate a solution; instead allow your Higher Source to come to the rescue!

Begin to learn to trust this great source who you have already opened the lines of communication with from last week's affirmation. This can be terrifying at the first attempt for you're used to being in control, even though this domination has caused you great misery. There's a saying – "when the pain gets too great I will surrender." Therefore, surrender your problems to a Higher Source and observe the results.

A word of warning; you may be tempted to jump back into the driver seat of your problems. When this temptation occurs, turn the reins back over to your Higher Source, and learn the lesson of waiting for the solution. After all the answer to your dilemma is often the one you least expect. Trust your Higher Source to resolve the issue.

. . . .

I am turning over my problems to my Higher Source as I learn to trust in its plan for the best results.

. . . .

WEEK FOURTEEN

EXPECT A SOLUTION

Last week, when you turned your problems over to your Higher Source, did you feel the freedom by letting it go? Or did you try to discover a solution? Drove yourself kooky by obsessing on your issue? Were you looking for an answer from people and/or the internet to no avail?

If you search for an answer and are obsessed on your problems, then you are blocking your Higher Source results. Your Higher Source will unravel the information in its own unique way in the perfect timing. Sometimes the problem is solved right away, although usually only time reveals what you need to comprehend. There are also occasions when there isn't an antidote; therefore, acceptance of what is.

Trust is the key to having your revelation of how to eliminate your issue. Answers can come in various forms: a book falls from a bookshelf, a song lyric you hear while doing the grocery shopping, a scene from a television show, overhearing another's conversation, an email, or in other words, any unexpected information that is received in an unusual way. Believe and you shall receive an answer.

• • • • • • • • • • • • • • • • •

I am giving my dilemma to my Higher Source, I am expecting a solution to happen the way it needs to.

• • • • • • • • • • • • • • • • •

WEEK FIFTEEN

INNER AND OUTER SPRING CLEANING

Ah! Spring makes you feel so alive! This season is a perfect time to let go of what we no longer need, while simultaneously cleaning those belongings we choose to keep. Which is why numerous people scrub their homes from top to bottom, while others focus on getting their bodies back into shape after the long winter. Yes, indeed, a spotless home and toned body are important; however, what about our inner selves?

Are you ready to let go of an addiction? How about improving your communication skills to enhance all your relationships? Could you be holding on to childhood or adulthood events which cause havoc in your daily life? Deep down inside you know what obstacles you need to remove. Spring is an awesome season to begin this process.

Another item that needs a tip-top cleansing are your dreams and goals; these always end up on the back burner. Get ready to dust off those projects so you can proceed back on track. Spring is a fabulous time to finish: writing a book, creating crafts, recording a song, tasting new recipes, doing research, and focusing on your dream business.

I am cleansing my inner and outer world.

WEEK SIXTEEN

THE GIFT OF CONFUSION

When you read that confusion is a gift, did you think to yourself, "How in the world can confusion be a gift? It's so frustrating to be confused." I agree having turmoil about an important matter can be frustrating; however, it's a sign that you are not ready to make a final decision yet. Allow yourself a time out until the answer becomes apparent.

If you are looking to make a career change that involves a relocation, it is normal to be confused. Do research on your new place of employment and the new area you could be moving to or talk to people who are knowledgeable on this subject. For matters of the heart, which could include getting married or ending a relationship, don't allow anyone to manipulate you to make a decision. Nor should you rush into making a choice before you are ready. Instead, get quiet, talk to your Higher Source, then be silent as you might receive an answer.

As you trust in this process, your clouds of confusion will drift away to allow the sunshine of your answer in. When the time is right, there will be no doubt of the right choice or direction to proceed in.

· · · · · · · · · · · · · · · · · ·

I am accepting my gift of confusion timing to bring the right solution.

· · · · · · · · · · · · · · · · · ·

WEEK SEVENTEEN

LISTEN TO THE WISDOM OF YOUR EMOTIONS

Have you ever felt confused on which way to proceed and couldn't form a decision on what to do? Think back to a time when you were unclear. How did you feel? Were you feeling: baffled, angry, desperate, heartbroken, lonely, jealous, or afraid? Your emotions are large clues on how to proceed.

There is wisdom in your emotions; however, don't allow them to rule you. Take the example of crimes of passion; if only the person had processed their feeling of betrayal in a safe manner, instead of acting out. In other words, pay attention to your feeling for a few minutes as you resist the temptation to react to it. Then, feel the feeling and allow it to dissipate. If you're still having problems with your emotions, instead of reacting, act in a grown up manner by: punching a pillow, expressing yourself in a journal, or speaking with a trusted friend.

To access your emotions to clear up confusion and to enable you to accomplish a decision, it is important to sit down, close your eyes, breathe, and go into your quiet space. When you feel calm and centered, allow one option of what you can choose to come to mind; how does it make you feel? Visualize what your life would be with that decision, what emotions come up? You can perform this with each alternative you could create. By doing this, you will know the right decision by how it made you feel: calm, peaceful, joyful, ecstatic, or it just feels like it was meant to be.

. . . .

I am listening to the wisdom of my emotions.

. . . .

WEEK EIGHTEEN

FACING FEAR

Some people say the acronym of fear is *false events appearing real*; however, other people fear everything and run. There are matters in life where it is extremely healthy to have fear as they alert you to danger. For example, being terrified when someone is pointing a gun at you is normal. Then there are other scary prospects in life that need to be faced; for instance, asking someone out on a date or a boss for a raise.

When there is something in your heart that you desire, although it scares you – you must confront your fear. Envision your goal in front of you, feel the fear, next breathe in courage, exhale fear, breathe in courage, exhale fear… Continue visualizing yourself proceeding toward your goal, ask your higher source to help you if panic arises, and observe yourself facing the situation with a positive outcome. Practice this meditation until you are ready to do this in real life.

It takes courage to face whatever it is that you're afraid of, yet there is freedom on the other side once you gone through the process. You could be turned down for the date or not receive a raise, but you could also marry this person or obtain a gigantic raise. The reality is, it's better to know the outcome, than not know, and years later wonder what could have happened.

. . . .

I am facing my fear of...

. . . .

WEEK NINETEEN

THE GIFT OF PATIENCE

For the questions of meeting a soul mate, getting married, finding a job, the right career, or whatever their desired outcome, my clients often ask, "When will this happen?" How they cringe when they hear the horrible "P" word – patience. Yet, is patience actually so awful? A wonderful analogy of trying to rush an outcome is using the example of waiting for a cake to bake. It takes a certain of time for the cooking to occur, although your restlessness makes the wait uncomfortable. Pulling the cake out too soon will either cause the cake to flop or it will be raw inside.

Let's use the example of a single woman looking for her soul mate to showcase how patience is a gift. Being impatient could make her appear extremely needy, which would turn off an excellent prospect. Or she might meet a man who she assumes is "the one," only to discover anywhere from a week to years how he undoubtedly was *Mr. Wrong.*

Patience in this case of the single woman actually helps bring in her soul mate. Instead of the woman focusing on when my true love will come in, she is concentrating on her life. Time will pass faster now that she's involved in her daily living. Meanwhile, as a result of her focus not being on when, "the one" pops into her life.

· · · · · · · · · · · · · · · · ·

I am allowing the gift of patience for the perfect outcome to happen at the right moment.

· · · · · · · · · · · · · · · · ·

WEEK TWENTY

DURING THE INTERMISSION

How easy it is to say that patience is a gift; however, the waiting can be the hardest part. Many times we want what we want right this minute! What are you supposed to do during the intermission while waiting for a new job, your business to become profitable, or your dream mate?

During your waiting time you have the choice of whether it will be horrible or pleasant. Being stuck in traffic could be distressing, especially if you're late for an appointment. You may choose to yell at the cars, beep your horn, or chew on your nails. Is that going to cause the traffic to move any faster? Of course not! To have a more pleasant time, put on music you enjoy, sing, converse with people in your car, and (only if it is safe to do so) call or text your appointment.

During longer intermissions of days, weeks, months, or years, concentrate on what's right in front of you, instead of what you desire to happen. This is the time where preparation comes in handy. Let's use the example of wishing your business becomes successful. Here's a list of action steps to prepare in the meantime: engage in research, take a course, network with other business owners, write a book, record podcasts, and build a following on social media. Groundwork passes the time while aiding a positive outcome.

· · · · · · · · · · · · · · · · ·

I am choosing to focus on being positive during the intermission while preparing for....

· · · · · · · · · · · · · · · · ·

WEEK TWENTY-ONE

RIDING THE BUMPY ROADS OF LIFE

In everyone's life there are disappointments, obstacles, and painful days. Wouldn't it be wonderful if our existence didn't require us to deal with those matters? Or would it? Imagine a world where we always were joyful, had no problems, everything went according to the way we wanted it, plus the weather was always perfect. If this actually did occur, human beings would be bored out of their minds within days, weeks, or months.

Disappointment detours you to take another path, which in turn makes your life more fulfilling. When blessings occur, they're sweeter, for you have tasted the letdowns of the past. Obstacles teach how to navigate through the rocky roads to reach your destination. Riding a smooth road is a life without learning, without growth.

On a painful day it could feel like you are walking barefooted on a trail filled with large chunks of glass; nevertheless, without those days you cannot experience the spiciness of life.

On those difficult days, please know this too shall pass. Do what you must in order to finish this one day: pray, meditate, write in your journal, allow the tears to flow, scream into your pillow, allow someone to help you, or discuss your woes with a person you can trust. Before you know it, the day has passed. During a trying time in the future, you can look over your shoulder to see how far you have come, and use those lessons of the past to step on the gas of today to steer towards the future.

• • • • • • • • • • • • • • • • •

I am riding the bumpy roads of today for tomorrow's smoother travels.

• • • • • • • • • • • • • • • • •

WEEK TWENTY-TWO

EXPERIMENT WITH NEW AVENUES

Do you feel bored? Are you doing the same old, same old? Feeling like you're stuck? Then it's time to begin a change by sampling opportunities like the following: cook a new recipe, take a class, exercise at the gym, attend a yoga class, learn an unfamiliar craft, volunteer at a cause you feel passionate about, explore a part of your town or another city you have never been before, or begin the baby steps to start what you have always been terrified to do.

Are you thinking I can't do that? Here come the excuses: I'm busy, I'm not old enough, I'm too old, I'm overweight, I'm out of shape, I'm not smart enough, or I'm this ethnicity. And the list of cop-outs continues… *I can't* is used as an avoidance; however, the heart of the matter is you are scared. Fear of looking foolish or failing.

Whatever you'd like to undertake, remember everyone else was a beginner at one time. Yet, how else can you learn anything if you don't attempt it? Think of this new undertaking as an adventure to become unstuck from where you are today. You never know, this could be the start of a wonderful journey!

· · · · · · · · · · · · · · · · ·

*I am enjoying experimenting
new avenues.*

· · · · · · · · · · · · · · · · ·

WEEK TWENTY-THREE

TAKE A BREAK TO KEEP STRIVING

Whether you're just a newbie or been at a project, hobby, or whatever for a while, when obstacles come up you might want to bail out. Don't! Take a break by focusing on something else, such as: breathe, meditate, go for a walk, watch an entertaining video, eat a snack, or vent your woes to a trusted worthy friend.

After you take a time out, whether that is a half hour or a week, when you do come back to whatever it was you were doing – you will view it from a fresh perspective. Whatever had frustrated you at the moment is no longer such an enormous deal; it might even seem silly now. Perhaps, your break enables you to observe just how valuable this project, class, hobby, life's work, or a new way of living is to you.

Many humans desire to become an adept at a skill without putting in the labor; however, a person turns into an expert with years of experience and work. At one point the expert was a beginner whose drive aided them to persevere at it daily, learn advanced information, work through problems, and rest when tired. The easy way out is to discontinue, although you will continue to grow old while wondering what if I continue…

· · · · · · · · · · · · · · · · ·

I am taking a break to keep striving.

· · · · · · · · · · · · · · · · ·

WEEK TWENTY-FOUR

MIRACLES HAPPEN

When I was in my twenties, a friend told me that she was leaving the state with another friend as her job was at a dead end, even after all her hard work. Unknown to her that so-called dead end place of employment was ready to reward her with not only a promotion, but also a hefty raise. Sadly, she gave up before the miracle occurred. Who knows how her life would have been different if she just waited a little longer?

My friend is not alone, since many people do this. For example, they begin, yet abandon: doing craft projects, writing a book, participating in a sport, playing a musical instrument, creating artwork, or something else they were gung-ho about when they first started. How tragic that they never experienced the rewards of achievement.

The next time you think of quitting,

hang in there instead, while pondering how much this project or situation means to you. Are you willing to accept future challenges? How much time or energy are you willing to put in? Can you be patient to achieve your goal? Would you prefer to feel the glory of accomplishment or just quit?

. . . .

I am willing to continue till the miracles happen.

. . . .

WEEK TWENTY-FIVE

REFLECTION IN THE RELATIONSHIP'S MIRROR

Relationships are where we humans get our greatest education is one of my most popular quotes. People relate to this quote due to the fact that some of our relationships can be extremely difficult. We can experience such disharmony, misery, sadness, or even joy when relating to other humans. Many individuals complained about the dysfunction of their mates, families, friends, co-workers, bosses, clients, or whoever is annoying them at the moment.

What many of us like to ignore is the reason we become educated from our relationships is that they reflect back issues, which we need to work on. An angry person is mirroring the anger within you, which needs to be released. Someone who oversteps your boundaries is teaching you how to set limits. They may also show where you need to be balanced, which is why opposites attract. For instance, a neat freak will attract somebody who is sloppy for both people to become aligned in cleanliness.

Would you like harmonious relationships? In the future when you're annoyed and/or ready to complain about someone, stop, and observe what they could be reflecting back to you. Is there inner work you need to undertake? Are you out of balance in a certain area in your life? What actions would aid you in achieving more loving relationships?

· · · · · · · · · · · · · · · · ·

I am paying attention to the reflection in the relationship's mirror.

· · · · · · · · · · · · · · · · ·

WEEK TWENTY-SIX

LET GO OF NEEDINESS

Are you single looking for love? Do you want more love with your partner? But has anyone told you that you're smothering them? It can be a double edge sword as it is a normal human instinct to desire having love shown; however, being obsessed with getting your needs met makes people run for the hills.

When you are feeling lonely, wanting love in your life, while not feeling good about who you are, it's like wearing a sign that says – my life is horrible and I expect you to make it better. Sadly, if you're single, only an unhealthy person will be attracted to your needy energy. For those of you in a relationship, more than likely your significant other will push you away.

Instead, love yourself, do stuff that brings you joy, and allow yourself to be filled with your Higher Source's love as well. For when you have both self-love and

Higher Source's love, the energy around you changes from neediness to being a beacon of love. This beacon will attract the right one for singles, along with improving not only your love life, but all the relationships!

. . . .

I am letting go of my neediness to become a beacon of love.

. . . .

WEEK TWENTY-SEVEN

INDEPENDENCE FOR LOVE

Did the title for this week's affirmation throw you off? After last week's affirmation you comprehended (hopefully) how neediness is unhealthy in all your relationships. You might be thinking that independence will be harmful to relationships. In a sense you are correct. When it comes to relationships and most things in life – balance is the key and worth striving for.

How many times did you hear or maybe even spoken these words, "He couldn't handle me because I'm too independent, which could be the reason our relationship wasn't meant to be." It may be this man was intimated by your self-sufficiency, although maybe you didn't allow him to do nice things for you that you are used to doing for yourself. Or pushed him away due to the fact he didn't think you needed him. Many men show their love by doing and helping; therefore, a woman who is overly self-reliant may cause a man to feel unlovable.

Too much dependence will make a man or anyone else desire to run away from you. What enables a healthy relationship is healthy dependency, yet at the same time giving space. Do what activates your happiness, take care of your responsibilities, and have your own life, while allowing your loved ones to provide you with loving assistance. Having your own identity can be a turn on, although allowing someone to serve you allows that person to show their love for you.

I am balanced in my independence in all my loving relationships.

WEEK TWENTY-EIGHT

SERVICE WORK

Have you ever been so wrapped up in yourself to the point of that you cannot observe other people in need? Maybe, you are grieving a loss? Perhaps, you're wallowing in the "should haves" from a past mistake? Or maybe you are fearful of the future? Instead of focusing on yourself – do service work.

How can you assist others? Here are several ideas for you: help out at a charity event, volunteer at a senior citizen home, foster kittens and/or puppies in your home, cook a meal for a person, babysit for worn-out parents, answer calls for a suicide hotline, pick up litter, or do whatever floats your boat.

Providing a helping hand keeps your mind off your grief, "should haves," and fears. It feels fantastic to notice you created a positive result for animals, people, or the environment. Who knows? You could adopt an animal or child, make a new friend, or even meet the love of your life. Often, when you are aiding others, a solution to enrich your life comes out of the blue.

• • • • • • • • • • • • • • • • •

I am assisting others and myself by performing service work.

• • • • • • • • • • • • • • • • •

WEEK TWENTY-NINE

NEW BEGINNINGS

Our lives are filled with chapters of new beginnings at different stages of our lives, for the sake of our continual growth. If we stayed the same throughout our lifetimes we would become stagnant or wither away. To flourish, we need to give birth to our next episodes.

Can't I stay the same? How frightening change can be! You may desire for things to remain the same; therefore, you struggle and fight the change. Or you are feeling impatient to have this transition come about, so you want to know when this will happen?

Think of new beginnings as a newborn child coming into the world. Instantly, the parents' lives are never the same with many changes such as sleepless nights, the terrible twos, or a rebellious teenager. However, they receive many blessings from the child. It takes time for the baby to learn how to walk, talk, and grow into an adult. Every new chapter in our lives brings permanent changes, imposes new lessons to learn, takes time for transformation to occur, and delivers enormous rewards.

. . . .

I am embracing new beginnings.

. . . .

WEEK THIRTY

ME TIME

Is your to-do list never ending? Are you running yourself ragged trying to accomplish everything? Do you consider yourself doing the work of two people? When you are focused only on crossing items off your list, on your next project, or on a goal, your thinking can become clouded or you could miss out on an opportunity. Your busyness usually will interfere with the joy of the moment.

Living in constant productivity causes stress, misery, and can affect your health. To avoid those negative conditions, take *me-time*. Instead of living for the weekend or vacation to rest and rejuvenate, fit in a mini vacation every day. Do your best to give yourself at least a half hour of *me time* daily. If a half hour seems overwhelming to you, start with five minute intervals, then increase it ten minutes, until you reach a half hour or even an hour.

Schedule *me time* in the morning, lunchtime, or before bed. For busy bees, exercise may seem the way to spend your personal time; however, do not use physical activity seven days a week. Instead, allow yourself to have gentle pursuits. Such as: reading, writing, meditation, naps, sitting in nature, or drinking a cup a tea while watching the world go by.

. . . .

I am making me time a priority every day.

. . . .

WEEK THIRTY-ONE

REASONS TO MEDITATE

Have you read articles that recommend meditation? Do you watch people meditating on commercials, television shows, or in the movies? Did you attend a yoga class where you mediated at the beginning of class, then you did this strange Savasana while lying on your mat at the end of the class? Did your doctor suggest you mediate for stress relief?

What is the purpose of meditating? Mediation is learning how to become quiet, to go within yourself, as well as a break away from your everyday life. The benefits of meditation are: you release stress, boost your immunity system, quiet the chatter in your mind, raise your self-confidence, and increase your ability to focus.

There are also spiritual benefits of meditation. When you meditate, it helps to keep you in the moment, develops intuition while opening up your psychic channels. You can develop a close relationship to your Higher Source by meditating. In rare moments, you will experience the incredible feeling of being at one with everything. Another reward of meditation is peace of mind. Are you ready to start meditating?

· · · · · · · · · · · · · · · · ·

I am willing to meditate.

· · · · · · · · · · · · · · · · ·

WEEK THIRTY-TWO

HOW TO MEDITATE

Many moons ago, I was on my landline phone with a spiritual adviser, and she mentioned meditation. "I don't know how to meditate," was my response. Then she told me to close my eyes. After a minute or two, she said, "You just meditated." Wow, you mean I don't have to climb up to the top of a mountain to mediate? Could it be that simple? Yes, it is!

If you assume that the only style of meditation is to keep your mind blank, you're incorrect; however, that is one form of mediation. Perhaps walking meditation would work for you? This is done by observing your feet; when your mind wanders you bring your attention back to your feet. Please practice walking meditation in a safe place.

Another way to meditate is to focus on an object, music, or your breathing. In Transcendental meditation you would chant a positive mantra over and over, such as, "I am love." Mindfulness meditation is when you are staying in the moment, what helps to practice this style is concentrating on the sensation in your body. For an easier getaway meditation, practice visualization. Close your eyes and observe yourself in nature, at your favorite indoor spot, or enjoying an activity. Experiment with different forms of mediation until you discover the one that is right for you.

. . . .

I am meditating...

. . . .

WEEK THIRTY-THREE

PRAY YOUR WAY

Are you like me that you weren't brought up in a religious household; therefore, you have no idea on how to pray? Or did you grow up in a home where you were dictated on the *right* way to pray? There's a popular belief that prayer is talking to God. With that belief in mind, if you're going to talk to God, would you speak words spoon-feed by another person or speak in your own words?

Some people believe that you can only pray for other people. I experimented with this (in the beginning days of learning how to pray) for my sister when I asked my Higher Source, "Please give my sister a break." Two weeks later, she booked a flight to Arizona on an airline that was having a special, "Buy one seat, get another one free." Since my niece was an infant, my sister could put her on her lap, and offered me the other seat. I was astonished how my prayer for her resulted in the benefit for me going on vacation!

Yes, it's proper prayer etiquette to pray for others; however, your Higher Source loves it when you're honest enough to pray for yourself. One of the most powerful prayers you can pray is, "Help me," for you're being completely vulnerable, as well as surrendering to your Higher Source. When you pray you don't need fancy language or formal prayers; instead, be yourself using your everyday words. There are no wrong or right ways to pray, only what feels right to you.

. . . .

I am praying my way.

. . . .

WEEK THIRTY-FOUR

BREATHE

In order to live, we are required to breathe air into our lungs. This sounds simple enough; however, countless people are breathing wrong. Have you ever paid attention to the way you breathe? Do you inhale and exhale through your nose or mouth? How deeply are you breathing?

When you're too busy to pay attention to how you breathe, most likely you're doing shallow breathing instead of inhaling and exhaling deeply. When you inhale and exhale deeply you're bringing life-giving air to your entire body and exhaling what is no longer needed. Other benefits of breathing deeply are: stress reduction, release of negative emotions, aid in digestion, reduction of wrinkles, reduced pain, and assistance in keeping the human body healthy.

To test how you are breathing, put your hand on your diaphragm to observe how it lowers when you inhale, and the way it expands when you exhale. If the abdominal area doesn't move much that's a sign of shallow breathing. Now, notice if you breathe through your nose or mouth. Nostril breathing filters the air, regulates the amount of air the body needs, prevents dry mouth, plus reduces snoring.

·················

I am breathing air deeply through my nostrils.

·················

WEEK THIRTY-FIVE

INHALE, EXHALE

In last week's affirmation, we talked about the power of your breath. Were you paying attention to how you were breathing last week? Was it difficult for you to breathe deeply through your nose? Or did you go back to your old way of inhaling and exhaling?

To integrate proper breathing into your life, the following exercise will aid you; however, it's important for you to focus on something that you perceive as negative first. Yes, you read that right, think negative. Reflect on whatever brings discord in your life: a person, a problem, your work, or a loss. What emotions are attached to this quandary: anger, jealousy, sadness, impatience, or fear?

Now, it's time to do the exercise. Inhale deeply the positive: love, peace, or healing energy. Exhale deeply the negative: person, obstacle, or emotion. Here's an example: inhale love, exhale anger, inhale love, exhale anger, inhale love, exhale anger, and inhale love… Continue to do this until you feel peaceful. When you perform this action it trains you to breathe properly, as well as to eliminate the negative in your life.

• • • • • • • • • • • • • • • • •

I am inhaling the positive, I am exhaling the negative.

• • • • • • • • • • • • • • • • •

WEEK THIRTY-SIX

FOOD YOUR WAY

How's your diet? Are you starving yourself? Do you binge on junk or fast food? Are your meal times according to the clock or when you're hungry? Who determines the food you eat: a recommended diet, dietitian, a person who cooks for you, or yourself? What types of foods are you eating when you're angry, unhappy, or frustrated?

There is no food plan that works for everyone; therefore, part of your journey is to discover what works for you. Don't expect to figure it out overnight, as it takes time and experimenting with different types of foods to know what works best for you. Make a list of all the diets or foods that you used to lose or gain weight while determining the following: did I feel better or worse on this food plan, how was my energy level during this time, what types of food were beneficial for my body, and was I satisfied with the foods I ate or did I feel deprived?

If you're still unsure, test your foods by eliminating dairy for a couple of weeks; however, allow yourself time to detox and adjust as it may feel uncomfortable at first. Then add dairy back in and observe how you feel. You can do this with any type of food category. To increase this a step further: process your feelings before you reach for food, only eat when you're hungry instead of allowing the clock to determine your meal time, and stop eating when you are full.

· · · · · · · · · · · · · · · · ·

I am discovering the foods that work best for me.

· · · · · · · · · · · · · · · · ·

WEEK THIRTY-SEVEN

INTUITIVE EATING

Did you know that your body knows the type of foods it needs? Your body shows you obvious signs that you are eating wrong with weight gain or loss, skin break outs, digestive issues, or illness. Another way your body communicates its fuel needs is through intuition.

What helps with this process is to become in touch with and listen to your body's intuition to discover the foods you need. Obviously, if you crave junk food or foods that have made you ill in the past, this is an addictive craving or using foods to stuff your feelings or problems. When you're hungry, ask your body what it needs to eat, or allow your intuition to draw you toward the foods you need to eat. You may have a sudden craving for a salad, fruit, or even red meat. Or be drawn to a certain item on a restaurant's menu.

The body lets you know what's lacking

in the body, regardless of your judgement. If you're a Vegan horrified by a craving for red meat, you don't need to eat red meat; nevertheless, your body is warning you it needs more foods with iron or protein. Instead of doubting the wisdom of your body's intuition, accept it, and eat the food it needs.

· · · · · · · · · · · · · · · · ·

I am listening to my body's wisdom by doing intuitive eating.

· · · · · · · · · · · · · · · · ·

WEEK THIRTY-EIGHT

PREPARE FOR LIFE'S STORMS

Life can seem like a storm at times. Sometimes you experience downpours or heavy winds. Other times it is hurricanes, tornadoes, or earthquakes. You might be tempted to hide your head in the sand as an ostrich does; however, your backside still feels the effects of life's storms.

Preparations are the key to survive adverse weather, as is foresight for your life's disruptions. How can you do this? To prepare for your personal storms, undertake the following: look within to know thyself, work on your issues, develop a relationship with a higher source, cultivate **safe** friends or family members, meditate, and take care of your body, mind, and spirit.

You are powerless to stop your life's storms; nevertheless, a strong foundation within yourself aids you to withstand it.

Staying calm in the moment will enable you to process clearly about what the next steps are you need to take: reaching out to a loved one, processing your emotions, or taking an action. By being prepared, you can navigate, survive, and become even stronger with whatever life throws at you.

· · · · · · · · · · · · · · · · · ·

I am preparing for life's storms.

· · · · · · · · · · · · · · · · · ·

WEEK THIRTY-NINE

DURING THE STORM

Life is like the stormy weather. Every so often we're able to predict it in advance, periodically we receive short notices, or on occasion it comes out of the blue. Just like Mother Nature, these storms can have minor or major effects on our lives. We have no control over the weather or events in our lives which bring on feelings of being out of control.

What types of events cause a feeling of powerless? The following are examples: loss of employment, death of a loved one, a tree falling on your home, imprisoned for a crime you didn't commit, victim of a crime, illness, or accident. These events are devastating whether you had advance notice or they were unforeseen.

Yes, you have no power on certain events; nonetheless, you *do* have control over your attitude empowering you with the ability to begin tiny or large action steps. If you were a victim of crime, report it to the police to avoid anyone else being duped by the criminal. Investigate medical and/or holistic treatments to aid in healing the illness. Whatever is occurring in your life, reach out for help to support you through these trying times.

· · · · · · · · · · · · · · · · · ·

I am taking action steps during the storms of life.

· · · · · · · · · · · · · · · · · ·

WEEK FORTY

AFTER THE STORM

Your stormy event may have lasted a few weeks, months, or years. Everyone weathers through life's traumas differently; some people may readjust quickly, while others take longer. Neither process is wrong; nevertheless, it is important NOT to stay stuck as you need to grow from the experience.

Please *ignore* those who tell you to just get over it and move on! You could do this easily if the crisis was stubbing your toe; however, more traumatic events take time. Allow yourself to: process your feelings, write down your thoughts, spend time with others who had similar experiences, or see a therapist. There will be bad days, although you could also experience good times, too. Anniversaries of the events may cause setback, which you will have to push on through.

These events will change you forever

and your life cannot return back to how it used to be. It may not feel like it today, yet know that out of horror can come beauty. You will discover your inner strength as well as new ways of living. Perhaps you made new friendships or learned something new? Life cannot remain stagnant; therefore, growth is inevitable. One day in the future, you may aid a person with the lessons you learned through your life's stormy time.

·················

I am growing after the storm.

·················

WEEK FORTY–ONE

HAVE FUN

Does it feel like all you do in life is work? How many hours do you spend doing chores? Yes, it is important to have a clean home, a career, and money in the bank, but that's not what life is all about. When a person's life is lacking fun, the following might happen: becoming bored, being lonely, feeling ill, or contemplating suicide.

Everyone has commitments and obligations in their lives; however, why not bring fun into it? Blast your favorite music to sing or dance while cleaning your home. During your work day, when speaking positively with your customers, clients, or co-workers, be engaging or use clean humor when appropriate. If you're stuck in traffic: play a game with license plates, dance in your seat to your favorite song, or create stories in your mind about the people in the car in front of you.

Allow yourself to do at least something fun once a day, which can be: read a comic, play with your pet, watch a humorous video, enjoy yoga poses, workout at the gym, or spend quality time with a loved one. At least once a month devote an entire day spent in fun. The benefit of being entertained is creating a life worth living!

. . . .

I am having fun...

. . . .

WEEK FORTY–TWO

PAY ATTENTION TO YOUR INNER VOICE

Do you ever have the feeling that someone you just met is dishonest, despite the fact a friend told you that person was trustworthy? Then later discovered you were right? Have you ever felt that you should bring an umbrella when it's sunny outside, yet dismissed it, and later were drenched when it down poured? How about wanting to kick yourself for not listening to your intuition upon discovering it was correct?

The above examples are what happens when you ignore your inner voice. Your inner voice can happen in the following ways: an inner knowing, an ache in your gut, a whispering in your ear, or a feeling such as creepiness or fear. It's easy to dismiss your intuition when there is no logical proof.

How can you begin to trust your inner voice? If you feel your innate knowing is giving a message, write it down in a notebook or type it in your smartphone - no matter how ridiculous the information may seem. This way you have proof if your intuition was right, as well as learning to recognize your inner voice in the future.

. . . .

*I am paying attention to
my inner voice.*

. . . .

WEEK FORTY-THREE

YOUR EGO VS YOUR INNER VOICE

In the beginning of learning to listen to their intuitive inner voice, plenty of people have a difficult time distinguishing their ego from their inner voice. This is normal as it always takes time to learn a new skill. One major clue that you're hearing your ego is when it gives guidance to harm others or yourself, which your inner voice would never do. The following explanations will help you determine whether it's your ego or inner voice.

Your inner voice will often come to you out of the blue in a flash-like manner. Its manner is so soft that you could easily miss it. Often, your inner voice intuition doesn't make any sense, which may create difficulty in trusting the information it's supplying you. When you do hear your inner voice and take action on the guidance, it is usually spot on.

Ego is the exact opposite of your inner voice. Your ego continues to yack away… It's so loud, that it is impossible not to notice. The ego has so many logical facts or explanations. "I'm right," demands your ego, "and you must listen to me." When you act on your ego, you often find the information was painfully wrong; however, it will defend itself till the end of time.

· · · · · · · · · · · · · · · · ·

I am learning to observe the difference between my ego and inner voice…

· · · · · · · · · · · · · · · · ·

WEEK FORTY-FOUR

ALLOW YOUR INNER VOICE TO GUIDE YOU

Once you begin to learn the difference between your inner voice and your ego, it's time to follow your inner voice. This is where the fear kicks in, "What if I'm wrong that it is my inner voice, when it's really my ego?" Well, so you made a mistake, which will enable you to distinguish this is your ego in the future – lesson learned. Please don't allow one mistake to deter you, whether it was a minor or major one.

To start you on your journey of taking action with your inner voice, experiment with the guidance of the little things, such as: bring an umbrella with you on a sunny day, take a different way home from work, attend an event that you normally wouldn't go to, or try a new type of food. A word of warning – there will always be someone who will tease you about your inner voice or tell you it's wrong. Ignore them and listen to your inner voice instead.

By practicing with your inner voice for the little things, it will enable you to trust your inner voice for more important situations. Listening plus taking action could enable you to: bypass a potential mate who is Mr. or Ms. Wrong, not lose an enormous sum of money in a business deal, avoid a serious accident or illness, prevent you from becoming a victim of crime, or save someone else's life. Do you now understand the benefits of listening and following the guidance of your inner voice?

I am allowing my inner voice to guide me...

WEEK FORTY-FIVE

DRAMA INVITATION

Are your relationships filled with chaos? Does disaster strike everywhere you turn? When was the last time you had peace in your life? If the first two questions describe your life or you can't remember the last time you felt peaceful, it's time to examine why this is happening.

If there is an enormous amount of drama in your life, you're allowing it! "What?" you may question. Take an inventory of yourself by asking the following questions: How much do you drink or use other mind altering substances? Do the majority of people you spend time with indulge in alcohol or drugs? Are your friends trustworthy or do they gossip about each other? If or when you're in a love relationship, is your mate loyal, faithful, honest, and treats you with respect? How comfortable are you during quiet moments with yourself or others?

Your answers to the above questions will determine how much drama is in your life; therefore, if necessary, you can begin to become willing to make changes in particular areas. For instance, if you discover the insight that the car accident you and your boyfriend were involved in was due to his heavy drinking. It's time to do deep soul searching about why you're with an alcoholic, plus ponder about how much you're drinking, too.

....

I am observing if whether or not I'm inviting drama into my life.

....

WEEK FORTY-SIX

STOP THE DRAMA

In last week's love affirmation, you determined how much chaos was in your life, as well as what areas. Then you began to become willing to change the causes. Now, it's time to take the action steps to stop the drama! Are you ready? Let's begin…

Ask your Higher Source to enable you to be courageous to take action. Here's an example to help show how to this. You may desire to point out to your friends how much they gossip; however, instead, observe how much *you* criticize people. By changing the way you speak about others, you're changing the energy from gossip to kindness, which could ripple out to your friends. If someone still continues to gossip, express that you feel uncomfortable about putting down this person. Then either say something positive regarding whoever was just slandered or change the subject.

In every area of life where there is drama do this: notice your actions first, begin to change your behavior, stop accepting other's inappropriate behavior, and speak up how a person's actions are affecting you. Remember, even though you choose to change doesn't mean that others want to. Can you put up with their flaws without any consequences, or will it stunt your growth? Obviously, if a person's actions are keeping you stuck in chaos, you must walk away from the relationship.

• • • • • • • • • • • • • • • • •

I am stopping the drama.

• • • • • • • • • • • • • • • • •

WEEK FORTY-SEVEN

AN ATTITUDE OF GRATITUDE

Is nothing working in your life? Are you always complaining about everything and everyone? Would you like to catch a break? Then begin to cultivate an attitude of gratitude. Being grateful is a useful tool to erase negativity from your everyday living.

A man I knew was extremely miserable; therefore, I would ask him to tell me three things he was grateful for. On some days he was grateful: that he didn't curse me out for asking him what he was grateful for, get evicted from his apartment, or was breathing. After a few months of telling me what he was grateful for, his attitude changed from being sarcastic to becoming more positive. This enabled him to discover the wonders of living.

What are you grateful for? During your

day, write, type, or say aloud what you are thankful for. It may be something tiny; nonetheless, what seems dinky to you is in fact a miracle. The miracle of: breathing, standing, eating, feeling, living, and loving! For an awesome life have an attitude of gratitude.

· · · · · · · · · · · · · · · · ·

I am cultivating an attitude of gratitude.

· · · · · · · · · · · · · · · · ·

WEEK FORTY-EIGHT

PHYSICAL BOUNDARIES

Are you wondering what a physical boundary is? Or do you think it's a fence surrounding a homeowner's yard to keep intruders out? In a sense, physical boundaries are similar to a fence; instead they protect our bodies. Here is my personal definition of what boundaries are from my book *Psychic Wisdom on Love and Relationships* - individuals set boundaries to feel safe, respected, and heard.

These are ways a person could violate your physical boundary: standing too close during a conversation, touching any part of your body, punching you in the face, or forcing you in an unwanted sexual act. Nobody has a right to touch you without your permission or in a way that makes you feel uncomfortable; however, it is your job to enforce the boundary before, during, or after the intrusion.

How can you execute a physical boundary? When you feel a boundary is needed, you can: hold your arms in front of you to stop an unwanted hug, block the perpetrator's hand or fist, use your voice by saying "don't touch me," or report a violation to the authorities. If a person reacts badly to you setting limits, please know it's appropriate to impose a boundary to ensure your safety.

· · · · · · · · · · · · · · · · ·

I am making physical boundaries.

· · · · · · · · · · · · · · · · ·

WEEK FORTY-NINE

VERBAL BOUNDARIES

Were you ever offended by words spoken by a stranger or loved one? Do you feel hurt when criticized by a person? Sticks and stones can break your bones, yet words have the potential to wound you deeply! Some people tend to brush off offensive or critical words as no big deal; nevertheless, in reality, these verbal statements are a form of emotional and mental abuse.

Examples of abusive speech are: why are you so stupid, you will never amount to anything, who would want to marry a fat pig like you, or why can't you be pretty like your sister. When a child or adult is spoken to in that manner, their subconscious mind doesn't judge the validity of those words while allowing them to be stored in the brain; therefore, those stored words will unconsciously affect their daily life in a negative manner. Now is the time to enforce verbal boundaries to those who use offensive or critical language.

You can make a verbal boundary by: telling the person you will not accept being talked to in that manner, letting someone know that this subject is not open for discussion, walking away from the verbal abuser, or asking yourself whether the source of the opinion is a healthy or a dysfunctional human being. After the incident, use positive affirmation to erase those harmful words. Lastly, vow to think first about what you're going to say to prevent you from speaking unkindly. Apologize immediately if you do blurt out critical or offensive words.

· · · · · · · · · · · · · · · · ·

I am making verbal boundaries.

· · · · · · · · · · · · · · · · ·

WEEK FIFTY

SPIRITUAL BOUNDARIES

Did anyone ever ridicule your religious or spiritual beliefs? Or try to force their beliefs upon you? How did you feel when someone pokes fun at your universal knowing? Perhaps you're wondering if there really are any ill effects when a person preaches that their way is the "only way."

Just like physical and verbal boundaries, spiritual boundaries are necessary to feel safe, respected, and heard. Since we're spiritual beings in human bodies, our spirituality is the source of who we are; therefore, it either enhances or has negative effects on our bodies and minds. There are numerous paths to a Higher Source, everyone has their own unique way of getting there; consequently, no person or religious belief is the "right" way.

When someone is shoving their spiritual knowing down your throat, the following boundaries could help you: disagree with them, listen without responding, take what the person said with a grain of salt, walk away from the discussion, or keep your distance. If a loved one threatens to abandon you unless comply with their religion or spirituality, this person is showing you that their love is conditional. Lovingly point out that you wish they could accept you for you are. If they cannot, then you are better off without the relationship.

....

I am making spiritual boundaries.

....

WEEK FIFTY-ONE

MOMENTS OF HAPPINESS

Have you ever felt happy? Do moments of happiness seem to elude you? Maybe you feel that joy is for others, yet not for you? Are you one of those people who searches for happiness? Repeat after me – I am worthy of happiness!

Humans often have the viewpoint that they should be happy all the time; nonetheless, that is impossible, for all our other human emotions need to be experienced to truly enjoy the feeling of happiness. Instead, savor the moments when you do feel joy. What are moments of happiness? They can be: feeling refreshed after a good night's sleep, taking a shower, watching a humorous video, painting the town with your significant other, spending time with family, talking to friends, finding your dream work, acquiring a new job or client, observing your pet, eating tasty food, learning something new, and the list is endless…

From now on quit, searching for happiness; rather than forcing it, allow joy to come in on its own. Sometimes you feel happy while serving others. Other times it comes when we least expect it. When you do feel joyful, stop analyzing it, or worrying how a tragic event will take it away. Enjoy the moment, enjoy the happiness.

· · · · · · · · · · · · · · · · ·

I am savoring my moments of happiness.

· · · · · · · · · · · · · · · · ·

WEEK FIFTY-TWO

CHOOSE PEACE

Have you ever felt peaceful? Do you crave more serenity in your life? The fifty-one affirmations before this one were designed to aid you to manifest a life filled with peace. As with last week's affirmation on happiness, peace cannot be a constant feeling; however, you can acquire moments of tranquility.

In your daily interactions you always have a choice to choose a response to each incident. Ponder for a moment on how you would react to the following events: dealing with a utility company, being cut off while driving, receiving the wrong amount of change at the store, watching your crush ask your friend out, or waiting for your partner when he/she is late and hasn't called. Those types of events could trigger a wide range of emotions, which need to be acknowledged, felt, and released, so peace may enter.

The following are ways to achieve tranquility: meditation, prayer, breathe deeply, contemplation on what you're grateful for, spending time in nature, reading inspirational books, listening to new age music, trusting your Higher Source with an issue, or asking yourself how important this situation will be in a week, month, year, or decade. Upon moments of serenity allow yourself to stay in the moment.

· · · · · · · · · · · · · · · · ·

I am choosing peace.

· · · · · · · · · · · · · · · · ·

CONCLUSION

Did you know that as long as you live, your personal growth path never ends? Perhaps it continues when you depart into the great beyond? There is no final destination when it comes to personal growth; therefore, enjoy the ups and downs of the journey. My wish is that this book has had a positive effect and inspires you to continue to grow…

If you could, I would appreciate it if you could leave a review at the bookstore where you purchased *Personal Growth Affirmations*.

Blessings,
Pamela Cummins

P.S.

I would love to hear from you and you can connect to me at the following places:

Website:

www.pamelacummins.com

Website:

learndreaminterpretation.com

Facebook:

facebook.com/PamelaCumminsAuthor

Pinterest:

www.pinterest.com/revpamelac

Twitter:

twitter.com/RevPamela

MORE BOOKS BY PAMELA CUMMINS

PSYCHIC WISDOM ON LOVE AND RELATIONSHIPS

Do feel like you will always be single? Are you sick of bad dates and relationships? Bored and unsatisfied in your relationship? *Psychic Wisdom on Love and Relationships* is a unique book packed with wisdom for BIG relationships. Go inside the world of a psychic to see how the spirit world gives knowledge to transform your love life. This book will take you on the journey of self-love, boundaries, intuition, communication skills, and more.

INSIGHTS FOR SINGLES: STEPS TO FIND EVERLASTING LOVE

Insights for Singles: Steps to Find Everlasting Love delivers insights to help readers reach their highest potential, learn to think positively, recognize red flags, how to let go of a relationship, improve communication skills, and understand how to *attract* and proceed with the "Right One." Whether you need to learn to "Keep your pants on" or "My fantasy is not reality," singles will find plenty of *potent* insight and *proven* solutions in this book.

PAMELA'S LOVE COLLECTION (FREE EBOOK)

What do self-love, the *Three F's*, and "He has to be spiritual" have in common? They are all in *Pamela's Love Collection*. Love is always in the air, but often it's just out of our grasp. It is time to start grasping it whether you are single or in a relationship. You will learn how to recognize the signs of healthy love and what to do with it. This eBook consists of twelve articles, blogs, and columns by love intuitive and radio host Pamela Cummins.

LEARN THE SECRET LANGUAGE OF DREAMS

Do you know that your dreams are special and unique? But if you don't understand their meaning, you are missing out on vital information. Because every night your subconscious mind sends you messages to help you solve problems, improve relationships, and teach you how to create a higher quality of life. The key is to learn how to decipher them and that is how Pamela Cummins, dream and relationship expert, can help you. *Learn the Secret Language of Dreams* is designed to give you the ability to understand the meanings of your own dreams.

Symbolism in dreams is not a "one size fits all." One symbol can mean many things. In order to understand the nature of dream symbolism more clearly, you will need to know what category your dream fits into. This book will help you identify the different dream styles so you can recognize what part of your life the dream message is for. Once you know the category of your dream, it will be easier to interpret your unique personal symbolism.

BIO

Pamela Cummins shows you how to empower yourself to empower your relationships. She teaches you to turn your dreams' nighttime messages into daytime wisdom. Pamela specializes in personal growth, spirituality, dream interpretation, and love and relationships. Learn more and pick up your **free** gifts at her websites **learndreaminterpretation.com** and **www.pamelacummins.com**

www.ingramcontent.com/pod-product-compliance
Lightning Source LLC
LaVergne TN
LVHW012010260326
834688LV00058B/631